salmonpoetry

Here and Gone

JOHN MENAGHAN

Published in 2014 by
Salmon Poetry
Cliffs of Moher, County Clare, Ireland
Website: www.salmonpoetry.com
Email: info@salmonpoetry.com

ISBN 978-1-908836-69-4

COVER IMAGE: *John Menaghan*
COVER DESIGN & TYPESETTING: *Siobhán Hutson*
Printed in Ireland by Sprint Print

In loving memory of my parents

GRACE REGINA GALVIN MENAGHAN
(1911-2000)

WILLIAM FRANCIS MENAGHAN
(1912-1998)

Acknowledgments

Acknowledgments are due to the following publications, in which many of these poems were previously published:

The Hopkins Review, The Recorder, Ginosko, nthposition.

"Living On" & "A Phone Box in Clonboo" appeared in *Spaces of (Dis)location*, Cambridge Scholars Publishing, Newcastle upon Tyne, United Kingdom, 2013.

What measure shall I give these generations
that breathe on the void and are void
and exist and do not exist?

SOPHOCLES

And if you ask how I regret that parting:
It is like the flowers falling at Spring's end
Confused, whirled in a tangle.
What is the use of talking, and there is no end of talking,
There is no end of things in the heart.

RIHAKU/POUND

Contents

I.

II.

I.

Done

She walks from the bedroom one morning, drops
down in her chair and quietly, firmly
declares: *I'm done.* You're what? my father asks
this woman who has spent nearly ninety
years bustling about houses, basements, yards.
She looks at him, a weariness accrued
over their marriage's half a century
flooding her worn-out body, eyes, and voice:
I'm done. I'll just stay here. From that time on,
my mother sits in the same blue chair, day
after day after day, no longer cooks
or cleans, rises only to make her way
to bed or the blue room, as she taught us
to call the toilet, a word she regards
as vulgar. Puzzling to me as a child
since it wasn't. Blue, I mean. Not a trace.

She's wrong. There's so much more to come. Before
she's truly done, she'll find herself sitting
in a pew at her husband's funeral,
in her same blue chair but moved to a new
Assisted Living room, in a strange chair
at a nursing home two towns away. Lying
not just alone in her own marriage bed
but on ambulance stretchers, nursing home
and hospital mattresses. And after
she's gone the mortician's gurney, coffin's
soft satin fabric, damp New Jersey clay.
But neither one knows that now as she sits,
her gaze less than serene, and says once more:
I'm done. Her husband, stunned at her stillness,
stands hoping someone will tell him, quickly,
what in the world she can possibly mean.

Till She Gets Back

Spring semester over at last,
I've crossed the continent
to visit my parents, only
this time needing especially
to see for myself how my
mother moves through her
days, or doesn't, since three
months back she plopped
herself down in her favorite
chair and declared: *I'm done.*

I've come, too, to do a few
days of research in New York
City, beginning tomorrow.
Now, though, I'm standing
with my father by the dining
room table, late at night, as
he prepares to join his wife,
asleep for hours, in their bed.
"You're doing pretty well,"
I say, "doing more things
for yourself, I mean, now
that Mom's no longer able
to do what she once did."

Since I arrived I've been
watching him, surreptitiously,
managing simple tasks in
the kitchen and such, passing
the austere hours of each day.
Remembering, and wondering
if he does too, weekend mornings
long ago when he made us all
pancakes on Saturday, bacon
and eggs on Sunday, giving
my mother a break from her
normal homemaker's routine.

"Oh, I'm just trying to keep things
going," he says, "till your mother
gets back to being her old self."
Before I can stop myself, I place
a hand on his shoulder and say:
"You know, Dad, I'm not sure
that's gonna happen." The look
in his eyes, bewilderment mixed
with fear, makes clear that's not
a thing he's let himself think.
At all. Till now. "I think she will,"
he says, his frail voice hollow, hoarse.
"Sure," I say, "anything could
happen." But I can tell he's lost
faith suddenly that the wife he
knew for more than fifty years
will reappear. I watch as he walks,
defeated, down the hall, opens
and closes softly the bedroom door.

The Fall

In a cheap hotel near Union Square
where the room's decidedly scuzzy
and the shower's way down the hall,
I stare, startled, at the greasy black
phone, pick it up on the sixth ring.
Hello? It's my nephew calling to say
my father fell last night. Is he OK?
"Just bruised, we think, but he spent
the night on the floor, calling for help.
Grandma heard nothing, slept right
through. I found him this morning,
face down by his recliner. We're
trying to get him to see a doctor,
but you know how he is." Jesus, if
only I'd stayed I'd have been there
to help him, I think, but say instead:
How bad is he? Should I come back?
"Your call, but there's nothing much
you can do, so you might as well stay.
Finish your research first, then come."

Two days later, the pain only getting
worse, he ends up at the doctor, learns
he broke his collarbone, finds himself
in a hospital bed—for observation,
given his age and all. The prognosis
is good, though we're told with old
people you never know. He jokes
with the nurses. They move him closer
to their station—to keep an eye on him,
they say, which could be affection
or concern. I'm afraid to ask which.
Back at the house my mother, not
up to a hospital visit, says very little,

passing the time almost placidly,
waiting for news. He seems to be
getting better, so on my stay's last
day I bid goodbye to my mother,
visit him on my way to the airport,
turn in my rental car, fly back to L.A.
It's the last time we'll talk face-to-face,
but I don't know that now. Instead,
the moment seems right for us all
to get back to our lives, after the fall.

Hold Me

I stand by my father's hospital bed
at the end of a long hallway, trying
to figure out how he is. A nurse comes
breezily through the door, does her thing,
nodding to me, saying to my father:
Is this your son? It is, he says hoarsely,
struggling to clear his throat. My little boy.
The nurse laughs. He's not so little, is he,
though, your little boy? I suppose that's true,
my father concedes. The nurse looks me up
and down, with just the faintest trace of lust
in her strikingly lovely pale green eyes.
I feel awkward, though, even noticing
those eyes, or how her gaze arouses me.
Are you all right? she asks. Or do you need
me to do something for you before I go?
I'm OK, he croaks. Would you like to dance?
She shoots me a questioning look. Dad, I
say, the nurse doesn't know what a joker
you are. You're fine though, right? For now, I mean.
Never better, he says. The nurse smiles, pats
his hand, gives me another look, and goes.
A look that says: And what can I do for you?

I'm still thinking about that look with a
sort of guilty pleasure minutes later
when my father tells me he needs to pee.
OK, no problem. Should I call the nurse,
or do you want me to help you up and
over to the bathroom? No, there's a jar,
a plastic thing somewhere, that he can use.
He can't, though, or at least he needs my help
not just to find the jar but pee in it,
which means I have to find his penis too,
and hold and aim it so the pee goes in.
A thing I've never done, or thought I would,

but need brings us this new intimacy.
More intimate, I think, as I hold him
than we have ever been. Then I reflect
that maybe, probably, when I still was
his little boy he did the same for me.
Was there for me when I most needed him,
as helpless then as he is now. I take
the jug away, screw on the cap, tuck him
back in. Bedclothes and blanket covering
his frail, aged, emaciated frame
that once possessed strength and vitality
enough to make four children with his wife.

Those days long past, there's nothing sexual
about his body now. He's still a man,
though. And if he once was a shy young boy,
these days he flirts, gently, with the nurses
who know such things mean nothing at this stage.
But what did that look mean she gave to me,
that green-eyed girl? I can't help wondering.
My life, I hope, being nowhere near over,
and though sans wife or child vital still.
And like my father less shy than I was
in younger days, though shy enough to feel
unsettled still by what I had to do,
or help my father do. This simple thing
he can't do on his own: pee in a jug.
His little boy. I am. Will always be.
Even after he's gone. But a man too,
whose body tingles at the memory
of those green eyes scanning me up and down,
their gaze taking me in and holding me
with some vague promise of a warm embrace.
He's drifted off now, breathing heavily
Aided by tubes from an oxygen tank
that keeps his lungs pumping but dries his throat.
He stirs, emits a child's forlorn cry.
I reach out, take his hand, and hold it tight.

Phatic Communion

The last time I spoke with my father
face-to-face was in his hospital room.
It was my last day in New Jersey,
and he seemed to be on the mend.
It was my last day in New Jersey
because he appeared to be improving.
I could have stayed longer, rearranged
my schedule, booked a new flight if his
condition had threatened to go downhill.
But he looked better now—after his fall.

Seeing the phone by his bed, I had an idea.
"Dad, have you spoken to Mom at all since
you ended up here?" My mother, too frail
to come for a visit, sat waiting at home.
"No, no, I haven't," he said, in a tone
hard to name. "Well, you must miss her," I said,
though after fifty years of marriage who
could say what either one felt—or wanted.
"Why don't I call her, then, so you can talk?
Wouldn't that be nice?" He looked uncertain,
but I punched in their number, pleased with myself.

My mother answered. All at once in my
mind's eye I saw her looking terrified,
sitting alone in her chair, dreading but
expecting too each time the phone rang
that the terrible thing had happened at last.
"Hi, Mom," I said. "No, no, everything's fine.
I'm just in his room with Dad and he wants
to say hi. Wait a sec. I'll put him on."

I handed my father the phone and stepped aside,
wandered out into the hall but stayed nearby.
Who knew what they might want or need to say?
So I gave them as much privacy as
the situation allowed. Not enough,
it appeared. In the soulless corridor
I could overhear clearly all he said.

But nothing I heard made me feel awkward
at all. You would think they were just old friends
shooting the breeze, comparing their dull days.
Accepting deep in their bones as simple truth
a quip I'd heard someone make: I can't complain,
and if I did who would listen? I'd laughed
when I heard it that first time long ago.
Yet now as I reappeared at the door
to check on him, and my father held out
the phone, saying my mother wanted me,
that quip felt not just true but searingly sad.

I spoke to my mother briefly, hung up
the phone, and sat back down beside the bed.
We talked about nothing much a while longer.
Then I needed to go if I wanted
to make my plane back to L.A. I wish
now I had stayed, not just that single day
but every day and night, there by his side.
I fled instead back to L.A.'s *Tír na nÓg*.
In two weeks time, my father would be dead.

Catastrophe

The tragic denouement, or unknotting, of a play or story,
the catastrophe often spirals outward and causes
suffering to those the hero loves or wants to protect.
From the Greek katastrephein: "to ruin, undo."

I.

the catastrophe

The call, when it comes, is not the first or last.
It's just the one that changes everything.
Before it other news, foreshadowing.
Plot complications: aspirated food;
talk of a feeding tube; peripeteia
when he takes a sudden turn for the worse.
Pneumonia leaving the feeding tube talk
far behind. Too late, all at once, to try
such bold device, dramatic intervention.

Come now. Move fast. Get here quick as you can.
No time to waste. It could be hours, days.
In high gear now, I'm trying to make it back
in time for the impending denouement.
I book a grievance fare, a rental car,
then pack my bags, remembering to bring
the dark grey suit bought months ago but not
yet worn. Time at last to don my costume,
assume my role in this catastrophe.

II.

often spirals outward

I make my way to the check-in desk,
explain my situation. The sullen
clerk looks up my reservation, then
tells me there's a problem. I can't
fly because the reservation must be
paid in cash. A credit card needs
twenty-four hours to clear. No,
I say, they told me on the phone
that I'm all set. My father's dying,
I say. He looks at me impassively.
There's nothing I can do. Then
get me someone who can, I hiss,
the menace in my voice so marked
a dozen heads in earshot turn and look.

What seems to be the problem?
another clerk asks. Problem?
My father's dying and this fool
won't let me on the goddamn plane.
Give me a minute, and I'll help you here.
I take one step aside, still staring hard
at my antagonist, letting the hate
stream from my eyes. And all at once
he looks as if he knows he's been a jerk,
but keeps his eyes averted from my gaze.
When the other has helped me at last,
I turn back to him and hiss: Asshole!
But my catharsis feels incomplete,
knowing as I do how much my mother
would condemn my using such language
—no matter the provocation—rebuke
my bad behavior if she heard that word.

And when at last, blinking nervously, he
raises his head and meekly bears my wrath
as if he were the victim of some crime
I've perpetrated, or might yet perform,
I suddenly see what a pitiful figure he is:
mere complication, minor character.

III.

and causes suffering

Boarding the red-eye I discover my seat's
on the aisle, yes, but in the last half-row,
with the toilet right across from me
and the flight attendants clustered
just behind in this slim, cramped tube.

Yet somehow this awful spot seems
right for the journey I'm taking: up
in the air all night, hurtling through
darkness, never knowing, from moment
to moment, if my father's dead or alive.

An hour in, nearly everyone's asleep.
But I sit wide-awake in the murk.
Thinking. Remembering. Wondering.
Fully alert, yet numb at the same time.
Dry-eyed, but wishing I could weep.

The flight attendants' hushed voices,
ghostly movements. A faint glow of tiny
lights. The muffled engine roar. And
running over and over through my head:
Hell at 30,000 feet. Or Purgatory? Limbo?

IV.

to those the hero loves

Before I collect the rental car I need
to meet my sister, flying in from
elsewhere on her morning flight.
She's not at the gate when I land,
but as I walk the long corridor
she comes into view, standing
on the checkpoint's far side.
She shoots me a little wave,
looking troubled but calm.

When I come up beside her,
though, she falls into my arms
and begins to weep. The airline
rep standing nearby looks
faintly alarmed. I shrug, raise
my eyebrows as if to say:
What's a man to do? Averting
her gaze, she leaves us to our grief.

Recovered and riding shotgun now
in the rental car, my sister insists
she wants to go home first, check
in with our mother. I want more
than anything to race to the hospital
while there's still time, or might be,
to see our father before he dies.
And it's my rental, she's my passenger.
But in the end I decide not to fight her
—as well as not to forgive her, ever,
if we don't make it to his side in time.

V.

or wants to protect

In the end, after a brief visit with our mother
we head to the hospital and find our father,
still breathing but in no state to talk, though
he seems to know we're there, hear the words
we speak despite not knowing what to say.

I want to stay with him from now until
the end, whenever that is, but no one
knows when that will be, not exactly,
though we're told it won't be much longer now.
Hours maybe, or days perhaps, but soon.

On the way my sister said she'd been reading
up on these things, and it turns out the dying
like to pick their moments, waiting sometimes
till the loved one gives in at last to that rumbling
in the belly and steps out for a quick snack.

The idea, I guess, is that your death's your own,
your last possession to share or not share
as you see fit. To spare or not to spare
loved ones and others from the memory
of that last moment, of that last, lost breath.

So "dirty stay up" as my mother calls me,
and still on California time, I say:
OK, I'll take the night shift then, so he
won't be alone if in the pre-dawn hours
he goes, gently or not, into the night.

VI.

tragic denouement, or unknotting

Alone in the dark by the bed, but not
alone, not really, my father asleep
beside me, if sleep is the word. More like
delirium, this sleep from which he won't,
most likely, wake before the end arrives.

In the neighboring bed a young man who
almost died in a motorcycle crash,
but when the doctor told him how close he'd come
to not being here he laughed it off,
confident of his immortality.

The young man's sleeping, snoring peacefully,
but my father's migrating back and forth
between agitation and calm. I reach
out my hand, speak to him softly, telling
him he's all right, though he's anything but.

From time to time a nurse, technician, or
orderly appears to check on him, on his
I.V., heart monitor, oxygen flow.
Vital signs anything but vital now.
And one, sounding amazed, says: "Wow, still here."

She means not me but my father, hanging
on another night after we were told
he might have only hours more to go.
When dawn arrives he keeps on breathing.
No change, or so it seems. My sister comes.

Half-whispering, we chat a bit. I go.
Step pensively into the morning light.
Meet my brother on the street. How is he?
The same. Then: Who knew life could be so strange?
We often differ, but now, sad-eyed, he nods.

VII.

from the Greek katastrephein

Help Me Up! my father calls out, struggling
to raise himself to a sitting position.
The tangle of tubes and wires trembles
as he moves, and I'm torn between helping
him rise and convincing him to lie back.

The third night, 3 A.M., dark night of the soul,
The spirit's journey from its bodily home
to a union with God. Full of hardships,
difficulties detaching from this world.
So St. John of the Cross described this time.

The soul's goal, he would say, to reach, achieve
the light of union with its Creator.
But what is mine, a skeptic at best, who
feels certain of nothing but that I don't
want my father to suffer? Or to die.

I slip my hand beneath his scrawny back
to hold him up, and feel his impulse fade.
Guide him back to the pillow, murmuring
reassurance, telling him there's no need
to get up, he just needs to lie still, rest

in the bed. But how do I know what he
needs now? And rest for what? For death?
So each time he tries to rise I help him,
then ease him back once again, over
and over and over through the long night.

Only days later, after he's gone, will
it come to me. In his delirium
he thinks he is lying still on the floor
with his broken collarbone, calling out
for help to rise up, be made whole again.

But right now all I know is he needs me
to help him, body and soul, through this night
that, though neither of us may know it, will
be his last. All I know is he wants my
help. He's not ready yet to rest in peace.

VIII.

"to ruin, undo"

I'm sitting in my parents' living room
with my mother and brother when the call
comes through. My brother answers,
listens, raises his gaze to me and nods
as our mother looks down at the carpet.

My father's gone. This morning my nephew
relieved me at his bedside, and I said:
He had a rough night, kept wanting to rise
up in the bed, but he's hanging in there.
How much longer, I wondered, could he last?

My mother accepts the news quietly.
My brother announces he's staying put.
But I want to go, to see him. Who
knows why? Or why each of us reacts as
we do? I drive myself to the hospital.

It turns out the moment my father chose,
if he did, was one when his two daughters
sat by his bedside. A curious choice,
it seems to me, since one of them had been
for years on end now anything but kind.

And though we're brought together by our loss,
both sisters seem to understand I need
to sit alone a while beside my father,
or what remains of him, indulge my grief.
For now, at last, my turn has come to weep.

Holding his cold hand as his nails turn blue,
I recall the story he loved to tell
about the time when I was born. My mother,
recovering in the hospital saw
his yellow nails and thought he must be ill.

Afraid to ask, she'd kept her fears quiet,
and only when she got home did she find
the cause. To surprise her, my father had
painted the kitchen yellow. He was fine,
and I and my mother healthy as well.

My sisters reappear, and I force myself
to let his hand go, cease weeping, accept
he's gone. But how can I leave him alone?
It's he who's left me, though, for parts unknown.
At least, I hope he's still out there—somewhere.

His body, now just an aged ruin, lies
stiffening, and my sister, the good one,
tells me he took in one last shallow breath
but never exhaled. *He went peacefully.*
So why do I feel unknotted, ruined, undone?

Late last night, alone with him in the dark,
I'd whispered more than once: It's OK, Dad,
for you to go now. I know you're in pain.
I don't want you to suffer. It's alright
to let it all end here. I'll miss you, but

you don't need to linger, endure. Let go
if you're ready. I wanted, I think, to
be with him when he died. Did he not want that?
Did he feel the need to spare me that last breath?
One more thing about him I'll never know.

Two Wakes

When my grandmother died, my mother's mother,
I was in third grade. The funeral parlor
sat across the street from my school, and for
two days instead of going home I walked
from the school to the spot where Grandma lay,
looking better than she had in years, but
cold and dead. I sat in the back, far from
the corpse, and tried to keep out of trouble,
but between visitors kept my sad mother
company, and felt the strangeness not just
of the event, occasion but of being
in this weird, fragrant room rather than home.

Now the custom has changed. No afternoons,
and just one evening, for my father‘s wake.
But we're back in the same funeral parlor,
run now by the daughter, whose own father died
some years back. The sign's been altered to
reflect her hyphenated name. They've done
their best with Dad. He too looks better now,
though that just makes it seem some impostor
lies in his coffin. But it's him, of course.
And yet it's not. He‘s here, and yet he's gone.
And all I know of who he was lives now
solely, though vividly, inside of me,
while he lies still. At least, his body does.

When Grandma died, I felt enormous guilt
because I didn't miss her all that much.
A crabby old woman who once forced me
to bathe in the kitchen sink, making me
favor showers for the rest of my life.
But I miss my father terribly, sense
I'll miss him more and more as time goes on.

Already he's become for me a man
whose faults I love as much as his good points.
Faults? I hear him say, in mock surprise.
What faults? The priest is praying over him.
Yet I know, or think I do, he needs no
help to make his way through heaven's gate, if
such a place exists, and he does as well.
Though even now I cannot seem to pray,
I hope angels have met him on his way.

Passage Grave

I.

The same month I was born my father died.
Not the same year. Forty-four years later.
Never, though, have I felt more like his helpless
child than now, as I stand and say my last
goodbye in this funeral parlor. The lid
on his coffin's about to close forever.
Never again will I see his face or
hear his voice or shake his hand. Never feel
his shoulders beneath the arm I've rested
lightly there, as intimate as he let
me be, being Irish and Catholic and so
never quite at home in his own body
—except maybe playing tennis, or when
the ocean swept him up, brought him to shore.

II.

My mother sits in the very front pew
at Our Lady Queen of Peace. The church where
my parents, new in town, came to their first
mass nearly 50 years ago. Did she
ever in all that time, in some idle
moment, imagine this one? She who feared
in recent years leaving my father home
alone, as if her mere presence could keep
them alive, together, until the end.
The last time she saw him was the day
my nephew brought him to the doctor and
he was put in the hospital. Then she,
too frail to visit him there, sat at home
waiting for news. When bad news came she
took it quite stolidly, convinced perhaps
they'd meet again in some far better place.

III.

Delivering the eulogy I recalled
two times my father taught me how to be
someone who stood apart and knew his worth
and dignity were unassailable
by anyone outside himself. And then
I said how lucky we had been to have
him here among us for so long. And that's
when I first knew he was truly gone.
I looked up at my mother then and sensed
she'd not be long behind him. She stared back
at me impassively, inscrutable
behind her mask. I left the altar, went
to sit back down, and as the mass droned on
I stood and knelt and clasped hands absently.

Grief surged and swallowed me. I felt at sea.
Remembered how my father feared the tide,
made sure we did too, because undertow
had nearly claimed his life—long years before
he'd married, had four children, a long life.
All that might not have been. The miracle
of ever being born came home to me.

IV.

I'm standing by a grave where I don't think
I've ever been before, despite the fact
it's where my father's parents lie beneath
a headstone waiting for my father's name
to join theirs, and my mother's after that.
And even then there'd be two spaces left.
But neither one for me, I hope. I want
not to be buried in the ground but be
burned like old Beowulf on some tall pyre.
Or failing that, in some oven. And then?
Have someone cast my ashes on the waves,
return me to that place from which, it seems,
our species came: the ocean's liquid womb.

Though he was in his thirties when the war
broke out, my father served in World War II.
And ended up in London where he sent, received
coded dispatches, indecipherable
by lowly privates like him. Spent his spare
time taking dancing lessons from some girl
he still talked fondly of years later. Or
dodging buzz bombs Hitler sent each day.
So there's a flag draped on his coffin now.
The question comes up: who will take it home.
I will, I say, and everybody smiles,
since patriotic gestures never formed
any part of my character before.
Still, it's a piece of who my father was,
a part of his and so my history.

I can't remember all that happened next.
I know there were some flowers, prayers and such,
last words exchanged with those who couldn't come
back to the luncheon we'd be hosting at
some local restaurant. The coffin sent
below the ground but not yet covered up
with dirt, a pile of which lay to the side.
A climb back in to the black limousine,
a short delay, and then the slow drive to
the gate my father never would pass through
from now until the end of time. Unless
he had already fled, as he believed
his parents had. Not here. No, no. Instead
installed in heaven days ago. That's why
he never took us to visit their graves.
"Why would I?" he'd say when his wife complained,
"when they've already left for Paradise?"
I'm hoping he was right, has joined them there.
But as we drive away I'm picturing
—I just can't help myself—the gravediggers
heedlessly shoveling dirt, filling that hole
where all that's left of him on earth remains.

AfterImages

I.

After my father died I stayed behind.
I could have flown back home. Plenty to do
back in L.A., with everything on hold.
Instead, I stayed ten extra days and sat
adjacent to my mother on a couch
my parents had bought before I was born,
while she sat in her same blue chair. Across
from us, set at a rakish angle, sat
my father's empty chair, a recliner,
the last of several and least hideous,
where he would sit and read the paper while
ten feet away the TV glowed and blared.

It's silent now. And so are we, mostly,
my mother and I, through the long dull hours.
I stayed not to talk over everything
but just to ensure she'd not be alone
in these first days after the funeral.
She didn't ask me to, and no one else
seemed to think I was needed. But I knew,
or thought I did, it was the thing to do.
The trick: not leave her locked in solitude,
yet somehow not intrude upon her grief.
I'd taken on that delicate mission
although I felt bereft myself. Perhaps
because I did, and sensed that she would be
as much comfort to me as the reverse.

Or maybe I just needed still to be
in this house where I'd spent my first eighteen
years turning into the man I've become.
My father's presence, image linger still
despite the empty chair. I see him there.

Not literally. A ghost of memory.
My eighteen selves, or more, from all those years
I called this house my home appear as well,
though fleetingly, as if they feared to be
caught by me and interrogated while
I stared into their spectral eyes, inquired
just who they think they are, or who I am,
and what became of all they hoped to be.

II.

One night, after my mother's gone to bed,
I see my father rise up from his chair,
seize up and stumble, clutch his chest, and fall.
I hear him moan, and then the cry begins:
Help me up. Help me. Help me. Help me up.
I'm here this time, but helpless nonetheless
—because he isn't. Just this phantom shape
lying terribly still. Afterimage,
persistent vision, though I never saw
the real event. The night he fell he lay
till morning calling for someone to come
and raise him up. No Lazarus, he lies
in his grave now, his only human aid
the prayers of those who still (as I do not)
believe in prayer, although my parents both
labored to raise me a good Catholic boy.
A phrase he used once quite reproachfully
to protest my lost faith, apostasy.

And I'm no Jesus who can raise him up,
though I was once His pious follower,
and then His double, with my hair and beard
flowing beyond the bounds of decency.
One day my father told me that I looked
not like Jesus but Charles Manson, saying
"I used to see guys in the office and

think: Who would ever want to look like that?
And now my own son looks like that." "Oh, Dad,"
I'd say, "admit it, I look cool." He'd frown
and look away as if in scorn of all
that I'd become. And yet I knew that he
would never cease to love and value me
no matter what I did or failed to do
or how I chose to look. And sometimes too
he'd let his beard and mustache grow awhile,
then ask: What do you think? And I'd say: Cool.

He's still here now, in some form, watching me,
it seems, as I watch him and seem to see
him walk now safely down the hall to bed,
crawl in beside my mother as he did
year after year. At which point I would move,
sit in that chair still glowing with his warmth
I stare across at now. And leave empty,
because I know no comfort's there, his warmth
of body, spirit gone not down the hall
but back into the atmosphere, deep space,
or somewhere else, but irretrievably
lost to me, like that body rotting now
at rest at last above his parents' bones.

III.

Among my father's many quiet skills
his mastery at hiding Easter eggs.
Each year he had to give us hints galore
before we came close to finding them all.
And sometimes, in a place I'd swear I'd looked,
where his hints led me back by telling me
You're getting warmer I'd find the last one,
and think he must have used magic on me
to make me miss it, or to place it there,
after I'd looked, not moving from his chair.

IV.

It's June, a week after he died, and I
stand in the backyard and survey the lawn
sweeping greenly back to the neighbor's fence,
small garage like a punctuation mark
off to the right. Remember where he lay
so often in the twenty years between
retirement and death beneath the tree
that grew in the same years I did myself,
here in New Jersey, till it gave him shade,
protection to lie motionless and turn
all that had happened over in his mind.

The years too when he worked in that garage
and on the lawn and house, keeping things trim
and orderly—before he hired a kid
I'd grown up with to come and tend to things.
Remember the cellar he'd worked to make
a kind of extra room, then given up
at some point, leaving it three quarters done.
Down there a ping pong table gave us all
(except my mother) hours of exercise.
I loved to win, but howled when I lost
or missed a shot. And oh, when I first beat
my brother it was sweet. But when I beat
my father that first time it made me sad.

V.

Contention is better than loneliness.
A Gaelic proverb

We used to tussle at the dinner table
about the War, the draft, black activists,
Manson and his pals, the length of my hair.
I drove him crazy saying: You don't know

for sure Manson did anything. Were you
there? *Of course he did! Look at him.* Look at
me. Am I a killer if I look like him?
It's not the same. But you do look like one.
My mother would chime in: Stop arguing!
We'd turn as one in wonder, stare at her,
and I'd say: We're not arguing. We're just
talking. And my father would concur. Then
we'd turn back to our prickly tête-à-tête,
agree on nothing but to disagree.

And now, the war over, Manson in jail,
Obama President, and my hair gone,
none of those quarrels seems to matter much,
at least as far as who was right or wrong.
And yet I miss them, wish we still could talk,
only this time not like debaters but
about so many subjects seldom broached:
his childhood, his own parents, the time
he spent in the army in World War II,
his tennis playing exploits, all the jobs
he held, his schooling. Anything to help
me know him better who once thought I knew
better than he on nearly everything,
and know now just how little we all know
about ourselves, each other, life and death.

VI.

There's lonely, and there's lonely for someone.
And when that someone's vanished from this world,
you realize there's some loneliness endures,
and will endure, as long as you yourself
draw breath. Some desolation has no cure.

I'm packing to return to my own life,
3,000 miles from where I drew my first
breath forty four long years ago. I breathe
the air around me now, here in the room
my brother and I shared as little boys.

Before that, though, I shared it with my parents.
Their bed, my crib together those first years.
My sister says one has no memories
before the age of two. Yet I recall,
I swear I do, a night in infancy.

Wide awake, I lay in my crib and watched
as lightning flashed, lit up the room, and rain
fell steadily around the house. My first
memory, then, if it is one: a storm
pounding the home that sheltered us.

I like to think the others all slept on,
—my parents, three siblings, and grandmother—
while I alone kept watch, viewing the world
in terms of dark and light, safety and storm,
before I knew words for the things I felt.

What do I feel now, standing in this room?
I feel my father's presence still, but feel
more powerfully his loss and how that loss
has altered my life and the lives of all
my family in ways we've yet to learn.

I feel again a kind of infancy,
of having just been born into a new
and frightening world, but with no father now
to protect me, to help me find my way.
It's he, not I, who's gone away this time.

More memories in this room than I can hold
at one time in my brain. The other rooms,
too, full of images, events, remarks.
Too much to carry back to my home now.
I pack my last few things and close the case.

VII.

The time's come when I need to be back home,
though I already am. My own home, not
this spot where I was born and grew and learned
all I would need to leave it far behind.
Three thousand miles behind, traveling blind.

And yet I thought I saw my future spread
before me like a kind of golden path
I'd travel to success and happiness
my parents could not dream of for themselves
—or me perhaps. And I could see myself

so far from here I'd never make it back.
Or could I? Am I just remembering
my hopes and not my fears? Did I foresee
years of uncertainty, trouble, divorce,
the death of my best friend, feeling so lost

home—this home—came to seem refuge, defeat,
and staging ground for a renewed assault
upon the world? And the one place where I
felt I could always come back, always find
love and acceptance of me come what may.

Sedate, my mother sits in her blue chair.
I can't tell if she's glad to see me go
so she at last can be alone with grief
whose depths no one but she can understand,
or dreads the moment when I'll leave her there

wholly alone at last to contemplate
her husband's passing, what time she has left,
and what it all might lead to in the end.
"Well, time to go," I say. "OK," she says.
"I hate to leave you, but . . . " "Oh, no, no, no.

You have to go sometime." "You'll be alright?"
"I will," she says, so unconvincingly
I think my heart will break right there. Instead,
I smile and say, "I'll call tomorrow then."
"Tomorrow," she says, as if a new word

had just entered her lexicon, as if
this simple concept were so novel, vague
I might have said "I'll see you back on Mars."
Two years and two months on, the day will come
when, all tomorrows past, she too is gone.

I hug her, grab my bag, turn at the door.
"I love you, Mom," I say, forgetting all
those times such words had been beyond me, stare
one last time at the one who brought me here,
into this world, who won't be long behind

my father leaving it, I know somehow.
This old woman. My mother. Looking lost
and fragile. Time to go. So out the door
I move. All the way back I see her there,
sitting at home, alone, in that blue chair.

II.

Living On

After my father died my mother stayed
alone in the house they'd shared for fifty years,
living through parents' deaths and children's
births, childhoods, adolescence, adult lives.

I spent that summer far away from home,
teaching in Ireland, where Dad's father
and mother had been born, just a few miles
apart, in rural Mayo—Ireland's wild west.

My father never made it there. London
in World War II was as close as he'd come.
No desire to go, he'd always insist,
the same as his mother had before him.

My mother's mother, a Scots-Irish mix,
was born in Greenwich Village. Her father,
though, had come from Dublin, and she'd have
liked to see the place. But she never would.

She'd refused to leave my father behind
just to see Ireland. Now that he'd left her,
it was too late. The time had come instead
to ready herself for one last journey.

Meanwhile, in Ireland I reflected on
how it felt to be fatherless amidst
these people at once alien to me
and products of a common ancestry.

Though nearly everyone looked so familiar,
to them I was a foreigner, a Yank
whose "roots" they had no interest in at all.
All these Americans who think they're Irish!

I understood their scorn, yet every day
I saw head after head that might have been
my father's—in profile, from behind,
full-face—and longed for one last long embrace.

Three thousand miles away my mother sat
preparing for the end, day after day.
And if God wasn't ready for her yet?
Well, let Him take His time then. She could wait.

Assisted Living

In the fall, my mother moves to Assisted Living.
It's not her idea or mine, but it is what happens.
And now, her husband six months dead, finds herself
surrounded by strangers and miles away
from where she'd spent the last half century,
knew all her neighbors. In this place everyone's old,
dying slowly, or quickly, or waiting till they get
sick enough that assistance is insufficient
and a nursing home becomes their next to last abode.

At Christmas I visit and bring along from her house
some bits and pieces to render the room more homey.
When I ask how she's doing, she says: Better me than
your father. He would have hated to end up in here.
If it had to happen to one of us, better to me.
I wish it could be different, I tell her, but we
both know it is what it is, and the only change coming
is the one where she moves to the nursing home or the grave.

On Christmas day, my brother brings her back to his house,
where my sister, the bad one, shows up late with no gift.
She claims she forgot the gift at home, sending my brother
into a rage at her thoughtlessness—though it's nothing new.
Back at the little room now, where I've returned her
in my brother's car, my mother tries hard not to cry.
And then she's weeping, telling me to go, not wanting
for me to see her like this. But how can I leave her?

Why can't we all get along, she wants to know, meaning
the siblings. I don't know, I tell her, though that's a lie.
I know all too well the myriad ways we differ.
But it's not your fault, I say. Dad and you did your best.
We might all have done better, of course. I hold her
till she stops weeping. And we talk, in the end, about

happier times, and I tell her how grateful I am
to have had such good parents. Then I leave her alone
in her old blue chair, not in her own but the Assisted
Living room where she lives now, after a fashion.

Birthday Call

Summer 1999. And I'm back
teaching in Ireland again. The program
I'd created before my father died
seems now like one more bad idea I had,
now that it keeps me abroad for so long.

It's my birthday, the middle of the year,
as well as the day I turn 45.
Knowing that to remember and call me
may both be well beyond her at this point,
I decide to call my mother so she

can wish me a happy birthday. Hoping
the gesture will seem not self-regarding
but kind. A reaching out from far away
now that I mostly can't call, with no phone
of my own and an ocean between us.

In the time since my father died, I'd called
nearly every day, talking only for
a minute or two sometimes, sometimes more,
depending on the time of day, her mood,
how much I could think to ask her, or tell.

I'm standing in a kind of tunnel now
at the bottom of two facing stairwells,
a sort of echo chamber, using a public phone.
I insert a call card that buys me ten
pounds of calls, not knowing how long that is.

Tap in the numbers. After seven rings
she finally picks up. "Hello," her voice small
and uncertain. "Hi, Mom, it's me. Just thought
I'd call so we could talk on my birthday.
Is that OK?" "Oh, yes, I'm glad you did."

Then I tell her how glad I am she gave
me life. How much I miss her. What I'll do
for my birthday later on. Afternoon
here already, I tell her, almost night.

The wrong note to strike. She sounds confused now
about the time, the day. So then I say:
Thank you for having me. Meant as a kind
and vaguely compensatory remark.
For the time confusion, her labor pains,

the struggle to raise me well. To be a
good mother, whatever that means. To be
patient with me as I struggled to find
my own way through my world. A way and world
that she so often failed to understand.

Now that phone card is clicking down, so I
say, "Mom, I have to go, but I love you
and I'll talk to you again." "I love you,
too," she says. "And happy birthday." "OK, thanks.
OK, bye." Then all the minutes are gone.

And she is too. Too suddenly. And I
hope she understands what just happened, that
I didn't just hang up on her. To call
her back and explain, I'd need to go buy
another card. By which time she may well

have forgotten the whole call, my birthday,
where I am exactly. It's the first time
ever that I've called her on my birthday
and the last such day on which we'll speak.
One year on, she won't be gone—or talking.

A stroke will have taken her tongue away.
She'll have a new bed in a nursing home.
And I'll be back in L.A. Uncertain
how long she has. How best to observe my
big day—now that she has nothing to say.

A Phone Box in Clonboo

I.

A part of me thinks I should have gone home.
But for better or worse I've stuck to my plan,
headed west after my teaching was done
to spend three weeks in my friend's thatched cottage
writing about my Mayo ancestors.

Technically, I'm in Galway, not Mayo,
but my father's cousin lives just past Cong.
The two never met, and now it's too late.
My father dead for more than a year, while
Nellie still lives where his parents were born.

When I first came to see her Nellie claimed
God sent you to me, and I'd joked, saying:
No, no, Nellie, I came on the ferry.
What she meant, though, was my grandmother,
her Aunt Maggie, had sponsored her siblings

over to the States, while she, the youngest,
had stayed behind and so had never met
her aunt. Now, all these years later, God had
sent me for Nellie to spoil, and she'd done
an excellent job, acquitting her debt.

Each trip to Ireland since, I'd visited
her and her family. My closest links to
grandparents I never knew, and the place
that produced them. Though not on this trip yet,
making me feel just a trifle guilty.

And I'm feeling guiltier still to be
here at all when my mother's just spent weeks
in the hospital back in New Jersey.
Knowing I might have altered my plans, but
promised instead to visit in the fall.

II.

Now I find myself here at the crossroads
in Clonboo, a short drive from the cottage
where at night I hear rats run through the thatch,
providing an all too realistic sense
of all that my ancestors left behind.

The phone box a ramshackle wooden affair
whose door doesn't quite close all the way.
Hard to believe it's connected somehow
to the outside world, that I can just dial
and speak to my mother a world away.

I can, and I do, but when she picks up
I can tell something's wrong. I tell her where
I'm calling from, but she sounds far away
mentally, not just geographically.
So I'm not surprised when she says to me:

I'm sorry. I'm not feeling well today.
I'm not feeling myself. We'll have to talk
another time. Sure, Mom, I say, feeling
full of remorse I'm not with her right now.
I'll call again? *That would be better, yes.*

She hands the phone off to my brother then,
who confirms she's struggling a bit today.
None of us guessing she'll never quite get
back to feeling herself again. That fall,
she'll have two crippling strokes—and speak no more.

I step from the phone box into Irish
sunshine mixed with rain, feeling out of sorts
myself and much too far away from where
I was born and raised, where my true home lies.
The pub calls to me. But I head instead

back to the cottage where I'll be for two
weeks more. Sitting beneath the thatch, I think
how much she would hate having to live here.
That I should have gone home—while I still had
a home to go to, as the barmen say.

Different Strokes

I.

I'm planning my trip back east when the first stroke strikes.
I haven't seen my mother for more than six months.
Since my father died, she'd lived alone, then moved to
Assisted Living. I've spent a second summer
teaching in Ireland, a place she'd longed to go
with my father while there was still time. Now time seems
to be running out for her as well. Who can tell,
though, how much time she or I or anyone has?

This first stroke looked like the end, my nephew tells me.
The paramedics predicted she'd not survive
the trip in the ambulance. She did, though, and now
she lies in the same hospital where my father died.
How is she doing? I wonder. No one seems sure.
It's a miracle she's still alive, one doctor claims
—though miracle's not quite the word, it seems to me.
She could go anytime, he says. But so could he.

II.

When she seems to have stabilized I head back home,
having missed teaching some of my classes. Having
a life of my own that keeps going. Though I feel
just how fragile that life is too, with no guarantee
it'll last past tomorrow, today, a moment
more. My students, though they know why I've been away,
are mostly absorbed in their own concerns, want me
to be there for them, satisfy their needs, endure.

Two weeks later she's back in her room at Sunrise,
—the name of the place she lives now, although Sunset
would be more like it—when the second stroke arrives.
This time the damage is worse even than before.

Against the odds she survives again, but turns out
to be aphasic—to have lost the power of speech.
Aphasia, from the Greek *aphatos*, speechless, not
spoken, from *phanai*, to speak. Unspeakable fate.

III.

I'm staying at my brother's place in Hackensack,
one town away from where we all grew up. He sold
my mother's house, and then sold his, moved to this two-
bedroom in a fancy building looking down on
our old neighborhood from grand Summit Avenue.
My brother's windows, though, don't face that way. Instead,
as I stand on his balcony what strikes me most
are the many white steeples dotting the landscape.

Living down in the flat town of Maywood never
gave me this lofty perspective. The sleek steeples,
though lovely in a stark, plain way make plain as well
what a Protestant place this is. Not just this town.
America itself. A fact my thoroughly
Catholic upbringing makes it easy to forget.
And though I "fell away" from the church very long
ago, this austere array still takes me aback.

IV.

On California time, I stay up late each night.
But this time around, at his request, I'm leaving
the all-night vigil to my nephew. So instead
I sit in my brother's place and watch the Yankees.
Each night, it seems, they fall behind, then a late surge
gives them another playoff victory. Each night
my brother turns in early, positive they're doomed.
And the next day declares he can't believe they won.

He heads off to the hospital with my sister.
I wake late, putter about the place, make breakfast,
take a shower, walk the few short blocks to the bed
where our mother lies, her condition as stable
as it's likely to get. Until the very end,
we didn't really expect our father to die.
Now each day we're a bit better prepared for her
passing, yet every night she trounces Death again.

V.

One night years ago I stood at the kitchen sink,
drying the dishes one by one as my mother
washed and rinsed and set them, still dripping, in the rack.
I don't have my glasses, she said, *so if I miss*
any dirt just pass the dish back to me again.
But each time I did she'd grab it, irritated
at me. Or at her once semi-glamorous life
come to this: blindly scrubbing plates as age comes on.

And then, after a moment of silence to mourn
her lost youth and allure, out of nowhere, she asked:
What do you think happens to us after we die?
I almost dropped the big plate I was wiping dry.
Took a deep breath. Exhaled. I don't know. Nothing
maybe. Probably. *You don't believe in heaven?*
I don't think so. Or hell either. She slumped forward,
pulled the plug, watched the soap scum vanish down the drain.

VI.

My mother was only five when her father died.
"Nervous prostration" they called whatever he had.
He died at home, and was laid out in the parlor.
And eighty years later the memory endured:
the father she loved lying cold and pale and stiff

while family, friends, and neighbors invaded the house.
She never stopped hating the month of November.
It's late October now. Is her own death looming?

Her mother had died in the hospital. Will she?
My mother wished to keep her at home till the end
but Father Cooke had said no, insisted she do
everything she could to keep her mother alive.
My father'd agreed to having a feeding tube
inserted if it would help him to survive. But
if my turn comes, my mother said, I don't want that.
In her chart a defiant message: DNR.

VII.

A social worker comes by one day while I and
my sister are sitting by the bedside, watching
my mother manage her slow decline. Into death,
or so we think. This woman's seen the DNR,
and isn't happy. We step out into the hall
to talk with her. She speaks to us as if we were
children who didn't understand. You know, she says,
your mother will starve to death if you don't help her.

A choice we've already agonized over once.
By authorizing the doctors to shove a tube
down her throat, one they will likely never remove,
we can keep her nourished, alive. But to what end?
That's not what she wanted, my sister says, her voice
icy. When the woman persists, my sister looks
like she might just see to it this self-righteous bitch
dies first. So I step in, thank her, send her on her way.

VIII.

Aspiration: 1. Ambition; 2. Expulsion
of breath in speech; 3. Suction; 4. Inhalation;
5. Inflammation of lungs and bronchial tubes
from breathing in foreign material; 6. The
friction of released breath; 7. Will to achieve.
My father surprised us all by wanting the tube.
But then he aspirated so much food he
died of pneumonia before they could put it in.

Now my mother's highest aspiration, it seems,
is to be left to die in peace, or at least as close
to peace as you can come given her condition.
Speech being beyond her now, we can only hope
she hasn't changed her mind, as her husband had done.
But her chance to achieve that end, to leave this life
on her own terms, will have to wait. A week later
she's back in the nursing home, with no end in sight.

Nothing Good

As the months pass, my mother seems to settle in
to her room at the nursing home, a new routine
where all illusion of homeyness disappears
and the lingering question is how long she'll last.

I think about going back for the holidays,
but my brother says I'd be doing it for me,
not her. In her present state, mute and confused,
one day pretty much blurs into another.

He keeps us informed with what little news there is
through frequent emails and the occasional call.
After my father died, I'd phoned my mother more
than I ever had before. But that time's gone now.

I could still call and talk to her, but not *with* her.
Since the stroke left her speechless, she'd seemed to embark
on not just a second childhood but a slow march
back through youth, infancy, birth toward some pre-born state.

My sister calls me, mentions a friend whose mother
has lingered at death's threshold nearly twenty years.
Which would be worse for our mother? How can we know?
Should we wish her more life, more time—or a speedy end?

One thing is clear, anyway, my sister declares:
Nothing good can happen now. And she's right, I guess,
but hearing her say it aloud makes things all too plain:
no matter how far off it proves, the end is near.

After that call, I stand alone in the kitchen
missing my mother terribly even though she
isn't gone yet, and we'd often disagreed, and
I'd struggled to free myself from her vexing ways.

On a wall in the house we grew up in, now sold,
lived in by strangers, my sister hung a poster
that read: Nothing good happens fast. Now our mother
lies in her nursing home bed waiting for the end

while her patient husband waits in the grave. And I,
the last child she gave life? I don't know what to want
—for her sake or mine. All I know is she's come to
the point when nothing good can happen, nothing at all.

The Reason for Living

The reason for living is to get ready
to stay dead a long time.

WILLIAM FAULKNER

If everything that happens happens for a reason,
there must be some reason my mother's still alive.
This reason thing was her stab at wisdom, words she
applied like a salve whenever misfortune struck.

Now, eight months past a stroke that left her speechless,
she lies in the bed and laughs at my silly jokes,
while my niece laughs along at the other side of
the bed. I've brought this niece 3,000 miles to see

my mother one last time, to say goodbye. But not
explicitly, of course, since no one's talking yet
about the end, which may be far off still, or not.
Talk as we may, of death we say nothing at all.

But at some point, alone with my mother again,
as I had been so many times before, after
my siblings had fled, and before I did, privy
to so much my mother needed to tell someone,

I seize the moment—or perhaps stumble toward it—
and find myself saying: Well, we all have to die.
Even now I can't figure out how or why I
thought, even for an instant, I ought to say that.

But I'll always remember the look she gave me
then, a strange mixture of outrage and deep distress.
It told me, wordlessly, what a mistake it had been
to presume to speak about our common fate to her

when death was for me, or seemed anyway to be,
far off, while hers seemed nearer each minute, each day.
I'm sorry, I told her. I shouldn't have said that.
Her face softened then, and she seemed to forgive me.

But I'll take that look with me to my own deathbed.
And what I've thought since is: She never was ready
to die at all. Never mind stay dead a long time.
Nor will I be, I suspect, when my time has come.

Before It's Over

The thing itself is horrible. But the worst of it
is all the other horror before it's over.

HENRIK IBSEN

I.

Late July, and once again it seems the time has come.
Perhaps. We've been through this before. Two times before,
in fact, and learned to hedge our bets. At least, I have.
So when the call comes telling me I need to fly
immediately three thousand miles home again,
I half expect this trip will prove yet another
from which, relieved but empty too, I'll head back home
to wait a little longer, while my mother stays
alive in her nursing home. And to make things worse
my ear's infected, and my doctor says I'd best
wait several days at least before flying if I
don't want to burst my eardrum. So I wait it out,
then fly back home at last, and find her hanging on.
As if she knew to wait for me, as patiently
as she had waited all those years for one child or
another, one thing or another. Knowing that
if some things never came, eventually the child
always did, wearing the disguise of an adult
full of his or her mature concerns. Each forgetting
how we'd once lain helpless in our mother's arms.

II.

Alive still, breathing still, but helpless to do more,
neither quite sleeping nor fully awake, she lies
on her back, resigned, it seems, to let go at last,
or surrender at least to the fact that her body,

which has housed her troubled soul for 89 years,
has had it, become a machine beyond repair.
But still she's in no rush, letting the days go by,
letting her children wait, waiting herself perhaps
for God to give her the word that her room's prepared.
He's ready for her move to His holy mansion.
Or is she held back by fear of the cold, dark grave?
Impossible for us to guess, or her to tell.
But somehow the nurses know it won't be long now.
There are signs, it seems. I don't want to know what they are.

III.

Go maigh. Go hainnis. I'm good. I'm terrible. I
so preferred the sound of the second phrase that each
time my Irish teacher asked: *Cad é mar atá tú?*
How are you? I replied: *Go hainnis!* Why, she'd ask,
in English. What's the matter? No, I'd say. Nothing.
Everything's fine. I just like the way that word sounds.
And now, for no reason I can discern, while I
stand by my mother's bedside the two phrases run
in sequence over and over in my head. *Go
maigh. Go hainnis. Go maigh. Go hainnis. Go maigh. Go
hainnis.* I'm good. I'm terrible. Then the question
repeating: Why? Why? Why? Why must my mother die?

Opening the Window

I.

Does it matter if we're matter merely,
or body and soul, divisible whole
united for a time before the soul
departs the body's jail? A bold escape,
since there's no certainty beyond the skin.
A liberation into empty air?

Perhaps there's much more to it all than that.
But how much more? Or if there's nothing more,
no soul at all, the body on its own,
and when that's done endless oblivion,
what's there to care about except what is?
No more or less to do than simply live?

II.

Here at my brother's place I'm half asleep,
drifting through breakfast, when the call arrives.
A wake-up call. And now the nightmare starts.
Come quick, my brother says. Mom's going fast.
Don't hesitate or you might be too late.
Five minutes later I'd have hit the shower,

missed the call. I don yesterday's clothes,
drive to the nursing home fast as I can
and find my siblings and my brother's son
around her bed. She's waited, it would seem,
unlike my father, for us all to meet
beside her bed to bid a last farewell.

III.

The others move away to let me get
close to our mother, take her hand in mine.
Then a nurse comes, and as if there could be
something important left for her to do
displaces me and checks the fading pulse,
then tells us all our mother's gone at last.

She lets the dead hand drop and makes her way
to the window, opens it, turns back, says
I'm letting her soul go, then disappears.
Leaving the rest of us to stare across
the still warm body at each other, down
at Mom, not quite believing what we know.

IV.

Silence, then murmured words, a last touch, kiss,
bending over what moments before was
our mother. Then that nurse comes back to say
the undertakers have been called. Too quick,
I think. They want the goddamn bed.
The others, though, seem ready to depart.

I need more time, I say. I'll wait till they
come by for her. It's silly, maybe, but
I don't want her to be alone just yet.
The others go. I promise to follow.
Then turn back to the bed. It doesn't help.
She's gone already too. I'm on my own.

V.

When the funeral guys arrive they're shocked
to find me waiting by the cooling corpse
of my dead mother. I just didn't want,
I explain, to leave her alone. *OK,*
the kinder of the two replies. *But now*
you might want to go. You can stay,

he explains, *but then you'll have to watch us*
put her inside this bag. There's a black thing,
like a sleeping bag but shiny, rolled up
on the gurney behind him. *It's something*
you'll remember, he adds, *for your whole life.*
We'll take good care of her. And so I go.

VI.

As I move down the hall and out the door,
my thoughts remain behind. In my mind's eye
I see two bored young men lift up the corpse
half-absentmindedly and stuff it in
the gleaming bag, their minds on mundane things.
How long till lunch? Who might they nail tonight?

Back in the car, I sit a moment. Then
it strikes me I don't even want to see
them rolling out the body to the hearse.
I flee this parking lot, this nursing home
I'll never see again. Drive past a house
no longer ours, and realize all I've lost.

More Bitter Blues

Bitter the tears that fall but more
bitter the tears that fall not.
IRISH PROVERB

I.

I couldn't stop crying when my father died.
Now that my mother's gone, I can't seem to start.
When she died, a nurse lifted the window sash
to let her soul out. She fled, it seemed, without
delay, scorning the worn-out body that held,
or held back, her soul more than eighty-nine years.

In former times the people I come from placed
lighted candles around the corpse, draped with cloth
all mirrors in the dead one's room, stopped all clocks
as if to illustrate the end of time.
Instead, we passed her body off to strangers
who did things to it we don't want to know.

II.

The church my parents attended for fifty years
is closed for repairs, so the funeral mass
takes place in the neighboring town in a church
none of us have ever before been inside.
I give the eulogy from a lofty perch,
and the priest, a cousin, speaks consoling words.

Outside afterwards a neighbor, whose father
died only months before, tells a funny tale.
A man, it seems, who broke into the line
of cars headed for the church got pulled over
by the cops. His father, once a Captain in
the state police, would have loved to witness that.

III.

As we bury my mother in the one same grave
where my father and his parents lie, I ask
myself whether or not she might have preferred
to be "with her own people," as the saying goes.
Did she see herself as belonging to her
husband's close-knit family. I suspect not.

Then I think of my ex-wife, remarried now,
with whom I thought I'd spend the rest of my life.
Will I even hear about it when she dies?
Or she about me, if my time should come first?
My parents are together now forever,
my ex-wife and I eternally apart.

IV.

After the funeral, we'd gathered at some
local restaurant and fed all the mourners.
We'd talked of things and people and times past,
the present and future my parents will
never see. Now the bad sister's here in
our brother's home. Will I see her again?

Not if I can help it, I think, though I know
hearing me say as much would make our parents
terribly sad. But they're gone now. And soon I
will be too, back to a life where she has
no place. From some we never quite part, while
others die for us before their bodies do.

V.

The night after our mother died my sister,
the good one, had a visit from her spirit.
Not restless exactly but not quite prepared

to leave behind the comforts of this world.
Are you cold? my sister asked. Would you like to
come under the covers with me for a while?

Silently the spirit slipped between the sheets
and my sister held what seemed to be her body,
trying to warm her perhaps for the journey
that lay ahead. *I have to go*, she blurted,
then rose suddenly from the bed. O.K., Mom,
my sister replied, and watched her spirit fade.

VI.

Were you scared? Someone asked after she told
that story the next day. Not at all, she said.
It was comforting. And I thought: Why didn't
our mother come to me as well—or instead?
My sister swore it was real, not just some dream
she'd had. Who'd care, I thought, if only she'd come.

There's an end to everything, including ends.
And what doesn't end endures, and life resumes.
And in a way even what's over persists.
Eventually, though, everyone goes home
—if they can—to whatever life they have left.
Time, then, to pack my things and disappear.

Heading Back Home to a Place Where I Don't Belong

Home is the place where, when you have to go there,
they have to take you in.

ROBERT FROST

I.

On the plane ride home our grievance fares
get my niece and me two aisle seats
separated by half a dozen rows.
A part of me wishes she were there
to talk with through the long journey home
but a part's relieved that I can sit
in silence and turn over in my mind
all that's happened, happening, still to come.

My father dead more than two years, my
mother just days. I'm an orphan now.
And though in one sense they live on
inside of me and in others, still
it strikes me once we no longer can
embody, enshrine their memory
then they'll have completely disappeared.
So much, then, for immortality.

II.

While I've been away, the neighbors were
minding my dog. He's aging, but healthy
as far as I know. Yet all at once
in midflight the knowledge comes to me
with dread and terrible certainty
that he too will die within the year.
I don't know it yet, but that fall he'll get
lymphoma, his poor paw swelling up

to four times its size before he goes.
The night before that day he'll lie
unmoving on the kitchen floor,
moaning so much I'll come and sleep
beside him, cradle him in my arms,
and in the morning carry him off
to the vet where men will take him from me,
then come and tell me he too is dead.

III.

After my father died, whenever I strolled
with my dog through the nearby walk streets
of Venice I felt some sort of presence
seeming to hover in the air. Was he there?
It comforted me to think so and
I talked to him ever so quietly
—about what I can't remember now.
I wondered too how much he now knew

about things I'd kept from him while he lived.
After my mother died, she appeared
in my father's stead, and when I asked
whether he'd be coming back as well
her silence told me what to expect.
When my dog died, I wondered if he
might take her place. But instead no one,
no dog. And soon I stopped walking there.

IV.

Now, though, as the plane hits the runway hard,
I know none of that, or what else may come.
I only know that I'm home at last
in a place I've never quite felt at home

and missing my parents terribly
whom I all too seldom went to see
when they still lived. Much too busy, it seemed,
living my much more interesting life.

My niece and I catch a cab to my house,
then I drive her home. Return to my place
and collect the dog. He's delighted
I'm back, doesn't care where I've been.
The neighbors, kind, say the right few words.
That evening the dog sleeps at my feet,
and nothing has changed for him at all.
But everything, everything's changed for me.

V.

My sister, after our father's death,
told someone how shocking it had been.
How old was he? her colleague inquired.
Eighty-six, she said. And you weren't
expecting him to pass away soon?
Well, but not quite yet, my sister explained.
Our mother's death less of a surprise,
but we still weren't ready at all.

Life goes on, they say. Until it doesn't.
My marriage died many years ago.
It felt like a death, somewhere deep inside.
Now my parents are gone. And I have
no children. Live on my own. Wonder
what my remaining years have in store
—here in L.A., land of surf and sun,
where every day I wake up alone.

VI.

What does it mean to live, to have lived?
How did my parents feel when their own
parents died? And those parents before
them, losing the ones who gave them life?
How will I feel if I die with no
child of my own, just as Yeats once feared,
with nothing but some "dumb book"? He knew
how vexed was that quest for immortality.

I took a picture once with a crappy
camera. My parents sit holding hands
under a lamp that stands between them.
They're smiling for me, and look content
on this night at least to be as one.
A happy couple, as their silly son
insists on preserving the moment.
That print's still here. In my house. Somewhere.

A prize-winning poet and playwright, JOHN MENAGHAN has published three previous books with Salmon Poetry: *All the Money in the World* (1999), *She Alone* (2006), and *What Vanishes* (2009). Four of his short plays have received productions in Los Angeles, and one in Omaha. One of those plays, *A Rumor of Rain*, was published in *The Hollow & Other Plays* (2008). He has given readings around Ireland and the U.K, in France and Hungary, at multiple venues in London, New York, and Dublin, and across the U.S. from Boston to Honolulu. Menaghan teaches literature and creative writing at Loyola Marymount University in Los Angeles, where he also serves as Director of both the Irish Studies and Summer in Ireland programs.

http://redroom.com/author/john-menaghan